GW00319473

Margaritas

Barbara Albright

**Andrews McMeel
Publishing**

Kansas City

Special thanks to my parents;
my husband, Ted Westray;
Rhonda Brown; Tom Grotta; and the
rest of the taste-testing crew.

Margaritas

For information,
write Andrews McMeel Publishing, an Andrews
McMeel Universal company, 4520 Main Street,
Kansas City, Missouri 64111.

Book design by Holly Camerlinck
Illustrations by Deborah Zemke

ISBN: 0-7407-1033-8

Library of Congress Catalog Card Number:
00-100437

Contents

■

Introduction

Simply uttering the word "margarita" often magically puts a smile on people's faces and transports them to a place, a party, or a time when life was relaxed, fun, and carefree. A veritable fiesta in a glass, the blending of tequila, citrus, and salt is a spectacular combination (not to mention intoxicating) that has made the margarita one of America's very favorite drinks, equally beloved by both men and women. Even though this book is teeny in size, the recipes have been tested and retested. (Hey—it's a tough job, but someone has to do it!) Tuck the book in your back pocket or in a kitchen drawer and you will always be armed with the precise instructions on how to put together a rainbow of flavors of margaritas as well as some delicious Mexican foods to enjoy with the drinks.

The Elusive History of the Margarita

As with all great ideas that have come into their time, the margarita's enchanting flavor combination was one that was probably being thrown together in several locations at the same time—the best guess being sometime in the mid-1930s.

Americans were already vacationing frequently in Mexico at the time and becoming more familiar with tequila, perhaps when they slammed back the crude precursor to today's refined margarita—the tequila shooter—a lick of salt, a shot of tequila, and a bite of a wedge of lime. Or perhaps the margarita was a small but inspired leap from the cocktail classic, the Side Car, which is made from cognac, Cointreau, and lemon juice.

Not surprisingly, there are many women (named Margarita, of course) who have claimed they were the inspiration for the margarita and there are many bartenders who maintain that they developed the drink for their girlfriend, Margarita. The truth of the matter is, we don't know the precise beginnings of the margarita's sparkling combination of tequila, orange-flavored liqueur, lime juice, and a rim of salt. This is one piece of history that will proba-bly remain a mystery forever and

perhaps the drink's elusive inception is just one more element that adds to its allure. Of course, we are all indebted to the creator of this celebration in a glass.

Cheers!

Discussing the perfect margarita while drinking margaritas can be a fun pastime. For instance, one contingent believes that a margarita should never be blended. If it is, they view this drink to be a slush, not a margarita.

Others want their margaritas shaken with ice and then strained and served straight up or neat. If this is your taste, go ahead. I myself like my drinks very cold all the way to the bottom. This requires a chilled glass and ice or sitting in a freezer while I drink it. I'll take ice, thank you very much, hopefully with a sandy beach not too far away.

In this book, the envelope has definitely been pushed and there is a rainbow collection of margaritas from which to pick. For each drink, I have given very specific instructions. However, it's *your* margarita and you should make it precisely the way you want it to be. If the recipe calls for blending with ice and you don't want a slush, well, simply shake the ingredients with ice and strain it into a chilled glass if that is the margarita experience you are looking for. If you don't want a rim of salt on your glass, leave it off.

In my book, there are some universal truths about what goes into a margarita. A margarita should have tequila, an orange-flavored liqueur, and lime juice. A rim of salt completes the picture.

Most of the libations in this book include these basic ingredients though I found several of the fruit drinks did not taste good with a rim of salt.

(*A note about ice:* In all of the recipes, I have used the word "about" before the amount of ice. Ice cube sizes vary greatly. Adjust the quantity to your taste. If you like blended margaritas, I strongly recommend that you purchase a powerful blender or ask for one for your birthday. While more expensive, they efficiently chop up the ice in the drinks. I guarantee that you will wonder how you ever lived without one.

Tequila

Tequila is now one of the most popular liquors in the United States. At first it was in vogue among the bawdy "shooters" set (a popular choice in youthful singles bars and among the fraternities). As this audience aged, they began to see the sense in sipping a perfectly mixed margarita. Taking this refinement one step further, there is currently a trend now to sipping ultra-premium aged tequila from snifters.

As with other fine-quality spirits, the use of the word "tequila" is strictly regulated, in this case, by the Mexican government. Tequila gets its name from the town of Tequila in the Mexican state of Jalisco. Tequila comes from the blue agave plants that are grown in very specific locations in five Mexican states, Nayarit, Michoacán, Guanajuato, Tamaulipas, and of course Jalisco, where most of the tequila is produced. The arid climate and the dry volcanic soil along with the inherent qualities of the blue agave plants grown in these areas give tequila its characteristic flavor. In fact, tequila comes from the Nahuatl Indian word for volcano.

The blue agave is genetically related to the lily; however, it is a succulent that has many qualities that are similar to a cactus. Long, stiff, swordlike leaves with thorns on the ends radiate from the center of the plant. They protect the precious starchy heart of the plant, called the piña. It takes eight to twelve years for the plant to reach maturity before it gives up its piña, which can weigh from 50 to 150 pounds. Harvested by hand, the piñas are packed full of aguamiel (honey water). They are sent to a distillery where they are cooked to release the sugars that are then converted to alcohol through fermentation and distillation. By law, tequila must contain at least 51 percent blue agave. The remaining 49 percent is frequently fermented sugarcane, although other products may be used. The moral of the story is that tequilas labeled 100 percent blue agave tend to be the best. (P.S. Agave is the Greek word for "noble" or "admirable.")

By law, there are four types of tequilas:

Tequila blanco, also known as white, silver, or plata, is unaged and bottled soon after distillation.

Tequila joven abocado, also called gold, is a tequila blanco with flavoring and coloring added, typically in the form of caramel. Legally, it does not have to be aged.

Tequila reposado must be aged a minimum of two months and up to one year, usually in wooden containers made of oak and sometimes redwood. This frequently gives the tequila a mellower character.

Tequila anejo is aged in oak casks for at least one year and often two to three years. This aging can give the tequila a smooth, elegant, complex flavor, often with hints of vanilla and spice. These are the tequilas that are frequently hand-crafted for sipping out of snifters and they tend to be more costly.

The recipes in this book were all tested with tequila blanco with great success. I'm sure other types would also work, depending on your preference. As you experiment, you will educate your palate and have a great time.

Orange-Flavored Liqueur

A margarita just wouldn't be the same without the spirited contribution of an orange-flavored liqueur. In addition to adding a hint of citrus, it adds a sparkle of refined sweetness as well. In the recipes, I have listed the type I tested with, but other orange-flavored liqueurs will also work.

Here are the varieties that are most readily available in the United States:

Cointreau was created in 1849 by Edouard Cointreau in Angers, France. It is a crystal-clear liqueur that blends both sweet and bitter orange peels before it is distilled. It has an appealing exotic bitter quality. It is considered by most to be one of the finest orange-flavored liqueurs and I agree. It also costs more.

Curaçao is the generic term for several orange-flavored liqueurs that get at least some of their flavoring from the bitter oranges grown on the Caribbean island of Curaçao. Most curaçaos are amber-colored, but there is a blue variety, and Cointreau is clear.

Grand Marnier is made in France by Marnier-Lapostelle. It is cognac-based and flavored with Haitian bitter orange peel, exotic spices, and vanilla. It is amber-colored and has a rich flavor.

Triple Sec is a clear orange-flavored liqueur made from both sweet and bitter oranges. It is fruity and sweet.

Limes

Limes are available all year long, but they are especially abundant and less expensive in July and August. Most of our limes are grown in Florida and a few are grown in California. Limes are similar in flavor to lemons, but they are usually more fragrant. If you can't find limes or those that you can find are miserable-looking, you can substitute lemons. For the freshest limes, look for those that are firm with a dark green skin color. Yellowish limes are not as fresh and will not be as acidic. As the limes age, the skin will show brown areas. These can still be used, but they won't be as good.

Salt

There was a time when salt was a bad boy in the nutrition world and people would order their margaritas without. Perhaps you are one of these people. I was for a while, but to totally enjoy the complete margarita experience of citrus and tequila, you need the salt. However, make sure you put only a very thin rim around the edge, not a big gloppy one that leaves you with a mouthful of salt when you take a sip of the beverage. Some of the fruit margaritas are better without a rim of salt.

In my testing, I found that kosher salt was my salt of choice. It's a little more interesting than regular salt. You can also try sea salt. I found that the cute little containers of "margarita" salt were often not wide enough to accommodate my larger-sized margarita glasses. Simply sprinkle the salt onto a flat dish and dip away. Cover with plastic wrap in between margarita-making sessions.

Serving Margaritas with Style and Pizzazz

Presentation is worth a lot when you are serving any one of the following drinks. Just like the party-in-a-glass that they are, it's worth dressing margaritas up for the occasion.

First, make sure the glasses are cold. Clear out your freezer (there are probably a few unidentified freezer-burned parcels in there that you are better off without) and make a space to hold some

glasses. A frosty glass looks great and makes what is inside taste even better. It shows you are a host who cares about detail.

These glasses can be margarita glasses, martini glasses, hurricane glasses, chunky blue-rimmed Mexican glasses, and even canning jars. There are many, many cool Southwestern-themed glasses, drink stirrers, and accessories. In fact, a margarita party basket filled with a set of glasses, this book, tequila, orange-flavored liqueur, limes, chips, and salsa would make a great gift for someone (obviously you can scale this down to fit your budget—it must include this book though!).

When you serve the drinks, don't forget the garnishes. Lime slices and wedges are obvious choices, but berries, melon balls and wedges, and pineapple spears are other great ideas. You can also use edible flowers. Put several items on a skewer or festive pick.

In each recipe, there are recommended garnishes, but don't be limited by my suggestions.

The Perfect Margarita

Here is the classic combination—in just the right proportions. I especially like it made with Triple Distilled Porfidio 100 percent Blue Agave Plata Tequila. (And I like their pretty blue/green bottles, too!) The directions are written for a margarita that is straight up and one that is frozen. Of course, you can put ice cubes in the glass before you pour in the shaken drink. Multiply this recipe to make more.

1 lime wedge, plus 1 wedge or slice, for garnish (optional)

Coarse salt, for dipping the edge of the glass

1½ ounces (3 tablespoons) tequila

1 ounce (2 tablespoons) Cointreau or other orange-flavored liqueur

1 ounce (2 tablespoons) freshly squeezed lime juice

About ½ cup crushed ice

Run 1 lime wedge around the rim of the glass to moisten it. Dip the rim into the salt to lightly coat the edge of the glass. Place the glass in the freezer to chill. (This can be done several hours ahead of time.)

Combine the remaining ingredients except the garnish in a shaker and shake to combine.

Strain and pour into the prepared glass. Garnish with a wedge or slice of lime, if desired. Serve immediately. **Makes 1 magnificent margarita**

Frozen Variation: Prepare the glass as directed. Place all of the remaining ingredients plus additional 1/2 cup of crushed ice in the container of a blender and process on high speed just until slushy. Pour into the prepared glass. Serve immediately.

The Designated Driver Margarita

While I was pregnant, I craved citrus and I was looking for the flavor of margarita without any alcohol. Obviously creating an alcohol-free margarita was no easy task. Here is a drink that has the icy limey qualities of a frozen margarita without the alcohol. If the gang is at your house, the designated driver should sip on these or tell everyone to bring their sleeping bags!

1 lime wedge
Coarse salt, for dipping the edges of the glasses
About 1 cup ice cubes
1 cup cold water
1 can (6 ounces) frozen limeade
2 tablespoons frozen orange juice concentrate
¼ cup freshly squeezed lime juice
3 lime or orange slices, for garnish (optional)

❀ Run 1 lime wedge around the rims of 3 glasses to moisten them. Dip the rims into the salt to lightly coat the edges of the glasses. Place the glasses in the freezer to chill. (This can be done several hours ahead of time.)

❀ Place the remaining ingredients except the garnish in the container of a blender. Process until combined and slushy. Pour into the prepared glasses. Garnish each glass with a lime or orange slice, if desired. Serve immediately.

Makes 3 virgin "margaritas"

Sweet and Sassy Margaritas

If you like your margaritas to be a little bit sweeter, these made with limeade are the perfect solution.

> 1 lime wedge, plus 3 to 4 lime wedges or
>   slices, for garnish (optional)
> Coarse salt for dipping the edges of the glasses
> About 2 cups ice cubes
> 1 can (6 ounces) frozen limeade
> ¾ cup tequila
> ¼ cup triple sec or other orange-flavored
>   liqueur
> ⅓ cup freshly squeezed lime juice

Run 1 lime wedge around the rims of 3 or 4 glasses to moisten them. Dip the rims into the salt to lightly coat the edges of the glasses. Place the glasses in the freezer to chill. (This can be done several hours ahead of time.)

Place the remaining ingredients except the garnish in the container of a blender. Process until combined and slushy. Pour into the prepared glasses. Garnish each glass with a wedge or slice of lime, if desired. Serve immediately. **Makes 3 to 4 sassy servings**

Margarita Punch

Here's a punch recipe to make ahead of time. Like a wine sangria, it gets better as the fruits stand for a day or two. If you serve it in a punch bowl, make sure to add ice to the bowl or pour it into a glass filled with ice.

3 cups water
1 can (12 ounces) limeade concentrate
1 can (6 ounces) orange juice concentrate
¾ cup freshly squeezed lime juice
¾ cup tequila
½ cup triple sec or other orange-flavored liqueur
1 orange, cut into thin slices

1 lemon, cut into thin slices
1 lime, cut into thin slices, plus 8 to 10 lime
   wedges
Coarse salt for dipping the edges of the glasses
Ice cubes, for serving

In a large container, such as a glass jar, stir together the water, limeade concentrate, orange juice concentrate, lime juice, tequila, triple sec, and citrus slices. Cover and refrigerate for a day or two.

Run the lime wedges around the edges of the glasses. Dip the rims into the salt to lightly coat the edges. Place the glasses in the freezer to chill. (This can be done several hours ahead of time.)

Add the ice to the glasses and pour in the punch. Serve immediately. **Makes about 8 to 10 cool libations**

True Blue Margarita

Blue curaçao, an orange-flavored liqueur, gives this drink its vivid blue color. Of course if you like your drinks straight up, you can strain the ice out of it into a chilled glass.

> 1 lime wedge, plus 1 wedge or slice, for garnish (optional)
>
> Coarse salt for dipping the edge of the glass
>
> 1¼ ounces (2½ tablespoons) tequila
>
> ¾ ounce (1½ tablespoons) blue curaçao
>
> 1½ ounces (3 tablespoons) freshly squeezed lime juice
>
> ½ cup crushed ice

Run one lime wedge around the rim of a glass to moisten it. Dip the rim into the salt to lightly coat the edge of the glass. Place the glass in the freezer to chill. (This can be done several hours ahead of time.)

Combine the remaining ingredients except the garnish in a shaker and shake to combine. Pour into the prepared glass. Garnish with a lime wedge or slice, if desired. Serve immediately. **Makes 1 magnificent margarita**

Merry Margarita

This rosy red margarita is made with cranberry juice. Its festive green rim is formed by dipping the edge into a mixture of sugar and finely chopped lime peel. It's a great drink to serve during the holiday season.

> 1 lime wedge
> 2 teaspoons sugar for coating the rim of the glass
> 1 teaspoon finely grated lime peel to coat the rim of the glass
> About 1 cup ice cubes
> ¼ cup cranberry juice
> 1½ ounces (3 tablespoons) tequila

1 ounce (2 tablespoons) Cointreau or other orange-flavored liqueur

❧ Run the lime wedge around the rim of a margarita or martini glass to moisten it.

❧ In a small bowl, stir together the sugar and lime peel. Hold the glass by the stem sideways. Using your fingers, sprinkle the mixture over the moistened edge of the glass to lightly coat the edge. Place the glass in the freezer to chill. (This can be done several hours ahead of time.)

❧ Place the remaining ingredients in the container of a blender. Process until combined and slushy. Pour into the prepared glass. Serve immediately. **Makes 1 extra-festive margarita**

Strawberry Margaritas

This frozen margarita is just the drink for those dog days of summer when strawberries are at their finest. It's the perfect drink to offer guests on the Fourth of July. For an All-American red, white, and blue beverage, garnish each drink with an American flag pick that is skewering strawberries and blueberries. Serve them with True Blue Margaritas (page 37) to complete the picture.

3 cups trimmed, cleaned, and stemmed
  strawberries
About 2 cups ice cubes
¾ cup tequila
½ cup Grand Marnier or other orange-
  flavored liqueur
½ cup freshly squeezed lime juice

Place the strawberries in a freezer-weight plastic bag. Freeze the strawberries until they are firm. Place 3 or 4 glasses in the freezer to chill. (This can be done several hours ahead of time.)

Place about half the frozen strawberries, half the ice cubes, the tequila, Grand Marnier, and lime juice in the container of a blender. Process until combined. Add the remaining strawberries and ice cubes and process until slushy.

Pour into the chilled glasses. Serve immediately. **Makes 3 to 4 berry delicious margaritas**

Frozen Watermelon Margaritas

These margaritas are especially sublime in the summer when watermelon is at its peak. It's easier if you use seedless watermelon, but you can also use watermelon with seeds and simply remove all of them.

---

4 cups of 1-inch chunks seedless watermelon
Several lime wedges
Coarse salt, for dipping the edges of the glasses
About 1 cup ice cubes
¾ cup tequila
½ cup triple sec or other orange-flavored liqueur

½ cup freshly squeezed lime juice
Lime wedges and/or wedges of watermelon
or other types of melon formed into balls
with a melon baller, for garnish (optional)

Place the watermelon chunks in a freezer-weight plastic bag. Freeze the watermelon until firm.

Run a lime wedge around the rims of 3 or 4 glasses to moisten them. Dip the rim of each glass into the salt to coat the edges. Place the glasses in the freezer to chill. (This can be done several hours ahead of time.)

Place about half the frozen watermelon cubes, half the ice cubes, and the tequila, triple sec, and lime juice in the container of a blender. Process until combined. Add the remaining watermelon and ice cubes and process until slushy.

🍉 Pour into the prepared glasses. Garnish with lime and melon wedges, if desired. Serve immediately. **Makes 3 to 4 marvelous margaritas**

Peach Flutter Ritas

Debbie Rutter Walt (a.k.a. Flutter) and I worked at a New York City–based public relations agency on a liquor account. Every once in a while, we'd go out after work and have a margarita or two and then go to a sing-a-long bar called the Duplex in Greenwich Village where we would belt out show tunes until the wee hours of the morning. I spent a lot of time in the agency's test kitchens working on peach-flavored recipes, and Debbie and the client spent a lot of time sampling them. In her honor, I have created this peachy keen recipe.

1 lime wedge
Sugar, for dipping the edges of the glasses,
   plus 1 tablespoon
2 cups coarsely chopped, peeled, and pitted
   peaches
About 1 cup ice cubes
¼ cup freshly squeezed lime juice
¼ cup tequila
¼ cup peach brandy
1 tablespoon granulated sugar

🍋 Run the lime wedge around the rims of 2 margarita glasses to moisten them. Dip the rims into the sugar to lightly coat the edges of the glasses. Place the glasses in the freezer to chill. (This can be done several hours ahead of time.)

🍋 Place the remaining ingredients, including the 1 tablespoon sugar, in the container of a blender. Process until combined and slushy. Pour into the prepared glasses. Serve immediately. **Makes 2 show-tune–singing margaritas or makes 2 girls-just-want-to-have-fun margaritas.**

Razboritas

This dessertlike margarita would be a refreshing finale to any Mexican-themed meal.

> 2 cups raspberry sorbet
> About 1 cup ice cubes
> ½ cup tequila
> ⅓ cup triple sec or other orange-flavored liqueur
> ¼ cup freshly squeezed lime juice
> 3 to 4 lime wedges or slices and/or raspberries for garnish (optional)

Place 3 to 4 glasses in the freezer to chill.

Place all of the ingredients except the garnishes in the container of a blender. Process just until combined and slushy.

Pour into the chilled glasses. Garnish as desired. Serve immediately. **Makes 3 to 4 razzle-dazzle margaritas**

Cosmorita Slush

Based on the trendy drink the Cosmopolitan, here's an icy mixture to keep on hand in your freezer, ready to be scooped whenever the occasion calls for it. Serve it in a stemmed glass or in a snow-cone cup as an adult version of the childhood favorite. It has a texture similar to a granita and you may want to serve it with a spoon.

2 cups cranberry juice
1½ cups orange juice
1 can (6 ounces) limeade concentrate
¾ cup tequila
¼ cup triple sec or other orange-flavored liqueur

Stir together all of the ingredients in a freezerproof container until blended. Freeze until ready to use. Scoop into glasses and serve. (Let mixture stand at room temperature for about 10 minutes to make it easier to scoop.) **Makes about 8 icy servings**

Tommy's Frozen Tini Rita

Born to have fun, Tom Grotta invented this martini one night as a salute to the margarita. Like a margarita, it is flavored with lime and orange but it uses orange-flavored vodka in place of the tequila. Serve it in a martini glass and when you enjoy it, make sure to say "*¡Salud!*" to Tom!

1 lime wedge
Coarse salt, for dipping the edge of the glass
1½ ounces (3 tablespoons) orange-flavored
vodka

1 ounce (2 tablespoons) Cointreau or other orange-flavored liqueur
½ ounce (1 tablespoon) freshly squeezed lime juice
1 cup ice cubes
Lime and/or orange slices, for garnish (optional)

Run the lime wedge around the rim of a margarita or martini glass to moisten it. Dip the rim into the salt to lightly coat the edge of the glass. Place the glass in the freezer to chill. (This can be done several hours ahead of time.)

Place the remaining ingredients except the garnish in the container of a blender. Process until combined and slushy. Pour into the prepared glass. Garnish the glass with lime and/or orange slices, if desired. Serve immediately. **Makes 1 dazzling Tini Rita**

Tale-Telling Tiger Tails

As I was coming to the end of the recipe testing for this book, I went home to Fremont, Nebraska, to visit my parents. I also got together with some girlfriends from the Fremont High School Class of '73. While everyone was a teetotaler at lunch, it was soon evident that a visit to margaritaville was our destiny for this particular Friday afternoon and Leta Fornoff, Libby Vance, and I retreated to Dianne Siebler's lake home. With their help, I added some finishing touches to several of the margaritas and then we developed this scrumptious concoction made with pineapple juice. En route to making this, we came up with a universal truth—bananas and tequila should not be mixed in a drink. During the hours we spent sampling margaritas, I also learned *many* things that I never knew happened in high school. By way of explaining the tongue twister title of this golden-hued beverage, our school mascot was the Tiger and our colors were black and gold.

About 2 cups ice cubes
1 cup pineapple juice
⅓ cup freshly squeezed lime juice
⅓ cup tequila
¼ cup triple sec or other orange-flavored liqueur
3 to 4 tablespoons sugar

Place 3 or 4 glasses in the freezer to chill.

Place all of the ingredients in the container of a blender. Process until combined and slushy. Pour into the prepared glasses. Or, to serve straight up, vigorously shake all of the ingredients together and strain into the prepared glasses. Serve immediately. **Makes 3 to 4 tattletale margaritas**

Sangrita

Here's the Southwestern relative of the Bloody Mary. This version's fiery tomato-orange juice mixture includes tequila. One classic variation of Sangrita advises the drinker to down a shot of tequila and then follow it with a spicy tomato-orange drink. In this version, the two are combined. This drink is well suited for brunch and might be a good choice when you are looking for "a hair of the dog." For extra punch, make it with Hot Stuff Tequila (page 67) and add Tabasco if you want it even hotter. I delivered a leftover test batch to Tom Grotta and

Rhonda Brown. They added ice to it and gave it a whirl in the blender. If you are a salt lover, you might want to give the edges of the glasses a rim of salt.

2 cups tomato juice
¾ cup tequila (or substitute Hot Stuff Tequila and only use enough Tabasco to taste)
½ cup orange juice
¼ cup freshly squeezed lime juice
½ small onion, peeled and grated
1 teaspoon Worcestershire sauce
½ teaspoon Tabasco sauce
Pinch of sugar
Lime, lemon, orange slices, jalapeño peppers, celery sticks, spears of jicama or cucumber, for garnish (optional)

In a large pitcher, stir together all of the ingredients except the garnishes. Pour into ice-filled, chilled glasses and garnish as desired. **Makes 4 to 5 fiery cocktails**

Hot Stuff Tequila

This infused tequila is easy to make and guaranteed to put hair on your chest. Store it in the freezer and use it in Sangrita (page 64) if you like. Or sip it straight up if you dare. Take this "infused-tequila" idea one step farther and try infusing tequila with other ingredients. For instance, add citrus peels, pineapple chunks, or strawberries to a jar filled with tequila and refrigerate for 3 to 7 days until the tequila is flavored to your liking. Strain into a bottle, label, and store in the freezer or refrigerator.

> **One 750-ml bottle tequila (scant 3¼ cups)**
> **About 12 whole jalapeño peppers, washed**
>   **and dried**

 In a large, noncorrosive container (such as a large glass measuring cup or jar), combine the tequila and jalapeños and set aside in a cool dark space for 2 to 5 days. Taste to see if it has achieved the desired level of flavor.

 Remove the jalapeños. Strain the tequila through a fine-meshed strainer if necessary. Pour the tequila back into its bottle and label accordingly. Store in the freezer or refrigerator. **Makes scant 3¼ cups Hot Stuff Tequila**

Awesome Guac

This makes a jumbo batch of guacamole, but it is always gobbled up faster than you might expect. A generous quantity of lime juice also helps keep it from turning brown. Of course, you can always cut the recipe in half. Store hard, unripe avocados in a paper bag to speed up the ripening process.

---

3 to 5 very ripe Hass avocados, peeled, pitted, and coarsely chopped (about 2½ cups)
Juice of 2 limes (about 6 tablespoons)
2 medium jalapeño or serrano peppers, seeded and finely chopped

---

¼ cup finely chopped red onion
¼ cup chopped fresh cilantro leaves
¼ cup finely chopped scallions
1 teaspoon salt

In a medium bowl, combine all the ingredients and stir. Taste and adjust the seasoning. Taste again and readjust if necessary. Store, covered, in the refrigerator. If the guacamole starts to turn brown on the surface, give it a stir before serving. **Makes about 3½ cups of addictive guacamole**

Jalapeño Tomato con Queso
(a.k.a. Mexican Fondue)

Here's an easy and cheesy dip that is sure to bring the party together. Serve it in a fondue pot and keep it warm. Or, if you serve it in a regular dish and the dip begins to cool and become firm, scrape it into a microwave-safe container and microwave it for 30 to 60 seconds, or until it is dippable again.

1 tablespoon vegetable oil
1 medium onion, finely chopped
2 garlic cloves, finely chopped
2 large tomatoes, finely chopped

2 medium jalapeño chili peppers, seeded
   and finely chopped
½ teaspoon ground cumin
Dash salt
Dash Tabasco pepper sauce
2 cups shredded Monterey Jack cheese
1½ cups shredded sharp cheddar cheese
2 to 4 tablespoons chopped scallions, for
   sprinkling on top (optional)

In a medium skillet, heat the oil over
medium-high heat. Add the onion and garlic
and cook, stirring frequently, for 5 to 7 minutes,
or until the onion is softened slightly. Add the
tomatoes, jalapeño peppers, cumin, salt, and
Tabasco. Cook, stirring occasionally, until most
of the liquid has evaporated. Stir in the
Monterey Jack and cheddar cheeses and con-

tinue to cook, stirring constantly, until the cheeses are melted. Sprinkle with the scallions, if desired, and serve immediately. **Makes about 2 cups cheesy dip**

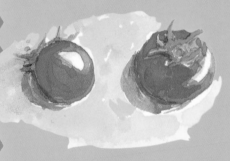

Sassy Southwest Salsa

*L*eave out the corn and black beans for a more classic salsa.

3 cups chopped tomatoes
1/2 cup chopped fresh cilantro leaves
1/2 cup chopped red onion
1/2 cup cooked fresh corn or thawed frozen corn
1/2 cup cooked black beans or drained and rinsed canned black beans
1 jalapeño pepper, seeded and finely chopped
Juice of 1 lime (about 1/4 cup)
1/4 teaspoon salt

In a medium bowl, stir together all of the ingredients. Serve with chips. **Makes about 4½ cups dip**

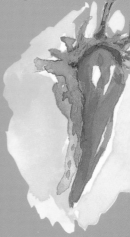

Homemade Tortilla Chips

Made-from-scratch (or at least from store-bought corn tortillas) chips are absolutely delicious and they make homemade salsa and margaritas seem even more special. Children are fascinated to see where chips come from.

Six 5- to 6-inch corn tortillas
Vegetable oil or lard for deep-fat frying
Salt
Chili powder (optional)

Cut each tortilla into 6 wedges.

In a heavy, large skillet, heat the oil or lard (at least 1 inch deep). Heat over medium-high until the oil is very hot and the edge of a tortilla sizzles when dipped into the hot oil. Add the tortillas, about 10 at a time, and cook, stirring very frequently for 45 to 60 seconds, or until lightly browned and crisp. Using a slotted spoon, transfer the cooked chips to several layers of paper towels to drain.

Sprinkle with the salt and then with the chili powder, if desired, while the chips are still hot. Serve soon. **Makes 36 extraordinary chips**

Heap a Nachos

Here's a recipe for a jumbo order of Nachos. Try making it with an assortment of different types of chips—there are lots of flavors.

---

9 ounces tortilla chips
1 cup chopped tomatoes
$1/4$ cup sliced scallions
$3/4$ cup sliced pitted ripe olives
$1/4$ cup sliced pickled jalapeño peppers
$3/4$ cup refried beans
2 cups shredded Monterey Jack cheese
2 cups shredded cheddar cheese

Preheat the oven to 350° F.

Place the chips in a mound on a jelly-roll pan. Sprinkle evenly with the tomatoes, scallions, olives, and jalapeño peppers. Add dollops (about 2 teaspoons each) of refried beans to the chips. Sprinkle the cheeses evenly over the surface.

Bake for 15 to 20 minutes or until the cheese is melted and gooey. Serve with guacamole, salsa, and sour cream, if desired. **Makes about 8 to 10 servings**

Chili Pita Crisps

Try these pita chips as a nice change of pace from tortilla chips. If you are in a rush, just make the pita chips and serve them with store-bought salsa.

Six 5½-inch white or whole wheat pitas
3 tablespoons olive oil
Chili powder

❧ Preheat the oven to 350° F.

❧ Split each pita bread horizontally into 2 rounds. Lightly brush the rough sides with the olive oil. Lightly sprinkle chili powder over the surfaces. Cut each pita round into 6 wedges.

🌶 Arrange the triangles on a baking sheet and bake for 5 to 10 minutes, or until lightly toasted. Serve with dips, salads, chili, or soup. Store leftover chips in an airtight container at cool room temperature for up to 5 days. **Makes 72 zippy crisps**

Mexican Puff Pastry Pinwheels

These puff pastry bites are a slightly more sophisticated change of pace from chips and salsa.

1 cup shredded extra-sharp cheddar cheese
1 cup shredded Monterey Jack cheese
⅓ cup finely chopped scallions
1 medium jalapeño or serrano chili pepper, seeded and finely chopped
2 teaspoons chili powder
1 puff pastry sheet (from one 17¼-ounce package frozen puff pastry sheets), thawed according to package directions
1 egg, lightly beaten

In a medium bowl, stir together the cheeses, scallions, pepper, and chili powder until combined.

Place the pastry on a lightly floured surface. Cut in half to form 2 rectangles. Using a pastry brush, brush one long side of each of the rectangles with some of the beaten egg.

Sprinkle the cheese mixture evenly over both pieces of pastry, avoiding the egg-brushed edge. Starting with the long side that does not have the egg on it, roll each piece of pastry jelly-roll fashion into a log and wrap each log in waxed paper.

Refrigerate the pastry logs, seam side down, for at least 3 hours, or until firm. (These can be prepared up to 1 day ahead of time.)

✿ Position a rack in the center of the oven and preheat the oven to 400° F. Lightly butter 2 large baking sheets.

✿ Cut the logs crosswise into ½-inch-thick pinwheels and arrange them, cut side down, 1 inch apart on the baking sheets.

✿ Bake the pinwheels 1 sheet at a time for 14 to 16 minutes, or until lightly golden. Using a metal spatula, transfer the pinwheels to a wire rack and cool slightly. Serve warm. **Makes about 40 pastry pinwheels**

Cheesey Beanie Wraps

These easy wrapped sandwiches can be heated in the microwave and are also great served as a cold sandwich. Cream cheese is flavored with scallions and cumin and spread over the surface of a flour tortilla. It is then topped with a refried bean and salsa mixture and shredded cheddar and Monterey Jack cheeses. I've kept the recipe simple, but you could also include finely shredded lettuce, cooked rice, chopped tomatoes, sliced olives, sliced pickled jalapeños, chopped green chiles, or strips of ripe avocado, shredded chicken, beef or pork, sour cream, or guacamole. In addition to making a great sandwich, you can refrigerate the rolls, and using a serrated knife, cut them into rounds that are each about 1 to 1½-inches wide for an easy hors d'oeuvre. Try experimenting with some of the flavored tortillas that are now available. If you are dining solo or perhaps as dos amigos, you can have your own little mini fiesta with margaritas and this wrap as a fairly substantial accompaniment. The recipe makes 2 servings, but you can adjust accordingly.

½ cup whipped cream cheese
2 tablespoons finely chopped scallions
⅛ teaspoon ground cumin seed
½ cup vegetarian, black bean, or regular canned refried beans

---

3 tablespoons salsa
Two 10-inch flour tortillas
¾ cup shredded cheddar cheese
¾ cup shredded Monterey Jack cheese

In a small bowl, using a fork, blend together the cream cheese, scallions, and cumin.

In another small bowl, stir together the refried beans and salsa to combine.

Using a small metal spatula or butter knife, spread the cream cheese mixture evenly over the surface of the flour tortillas. Then spread the bean mixture evenly over the cream cheese. Sprinkle the tortillas evenly with the two cheeses.

Roll the tortillas, jelly-roll fashion, around the filling. For a heated wrap sandwich, place the rolls, seam side down, on a microwave-safe plate and microwave on high for about 60 seconds, or until heated through. Serve immediately. For a cold wrap sandwich, cover with plastic wrap and refrigerate until ready to eat.

Makes 2 south-of-the-border sandwiches

Smoky Shrimp Quesadillas

Bacon adds an appealing smoky flavor to these substantial quesadillas.

---

3 slices bacon, cut into ½-inch pieces
1 cup chopped red bell pepper
⅓ cup sliced scallions, including the tender green tops
¾ cup ground cumin seed
1 pound small, peeled, and deveined shrimp (about 1½ pounds shrimp with their shells)
¼ teaspoon salt
⅛ teaspoon freshly ground black pepper
4 cups shredded Monterey Jack cheese

Four 10-inch flour tortillas
About 2 tablespoons olive oil, for brushing
 the quesadillas

In a large skillet, cook the bacon over medium-high heat, stirring frequently, until the bacon is cooked and crispy. Using a slotted spoon, transfer the bacon to paper towels to drain. Pour off all but 1 tablespoon of the bacon drippings.

Add the red pepper, scallions, and cumin and cook, stirring frequently, for 3 to 5 minutes, or until the vegetables are slightly softened. Add the shrimp, salt, and pepper and continue cooking and stirring for 3 to 5 minutes more, or until the shrimp are cooked through. Transfer the mixture to a bowl and let cool slightly. Stir in the cheese.

Place one fourth of the filling mixture on one half of each of the flour tortillas. Fold the plain sides over and press firmly. Lightly brush the tortillas with some of the oil and place them oil side down on a grill or in a skillet. Grill or cook them over medium-high heat for 3 to 5 minutes, or until lightly golden. Brush the tops with oil and turn and cook the other side for 3 to 5 minutes or until it is lightly golden. Serve with salsa, guacamole, and sour cream, if desired. **Makes 4 savory servings**

Chicken, Roasted Red Pepper, and Cheese Quesadillas

These delicious quesadillas are great as a meal or they can be served as an appetizer with margaritas. You can keep cleanup to a minimum if you grill the chicken and red peppers used in the filling and then grill the filled quesadillas, too. You can also cook the quesadillas in a skillet.

2 medium red bell peppers
4 cups shredded Monterey Jack cheese
3 cups chopped cooked chicken
1/3 cup sliced scallions, including the
   tender green tops
1/3 cup chopped cilantro leaves

Salt and freshly ground black pepper, to
    taste
Four 10-inch flour tortillas
About 2 tablespoons olive oil, for brushing
    on the quesadillas

Position a grill or broiler 5 to 6 inches away
from the heat source. Place the peppers on the
grill or broiler and grill or broil, turning frequently, until the peppers are charred. Place the
peppers in a bowl and cover. When cool enough
to handle, peel off the skins, core and remove the
seeds, and chop into 1/2-inch pieces.

In a large bowl, gently toss together the peppers, cheese, chicken, scallions, and cilantro.
Taste and season with salt and pepper.

Place one fourth of the filling mixture on one half of each of the flour tortillas. Fold the plain sides over and press firmly. Lightly brush the tortillas with some of the oil and place them oil side down on a grill or in a skillet. Grill or cook over medium-high heat for 3 to 5 minutes, or until lightly golden. Brush the tops with oil and turn and cook the other side for 3 to 5 minutes or until it is lightly golden. **Makes 4 savory servings**